AFFIRMING CATH

Kenneth Leech

POLITICS AND THE FAITH TODAY

Catholic Social Vision for the 1990s

DARTON · LONGMAN + TODD

KENNETH LEECH works as a community theologian at St Botolph's Project, Aldgate, East London, a centre for work with homeless people. He is also convenor of the Jubilee Group, a network of socialist Christians formed in 1974.

Fr Leech is not a member of Affirming Catholicism, and this booklet is a personal viewpoint.

© 1994 Kenneth Leech

Published by Darton, Longman and Todd, 1 Spencer Court, 140–142 Wandsworth High Street, London SW18 4JJ, in association with Affirming Catholicism, St Mary-le-Bow, Cheapside, London EC2V 6AU.

ISBN 0–232–52080–1

Booklets designed by Bet Ayer, phototypeset by Intype, London and printed by Halstan and Co Ltd, Amersham, Bucks.

CONTENTS

Affirming Catholicism

Affirming Catholicism has never been, and is not intended to be, yet another 'party' within the Church of England or the Anglican Communion but rather a movement of encouragement and hope.

A group of lay people and clergy met together in 1990 to identify that authentic Catholic tradition within the Church which appeared to be under threat. Wider support was expressed at a public meeting on 9 June 1990 in London and at a residential conference in York in July 1991.

Since then Affirming Catholicism has been afforded charitable status. The following statement is extracted from the Trust Deed:

> It is the conviction of many that a respect for scholarship and free enquiry has been character-istic of the Church of England and of the Churches of the wider Anglican Communion from earliest times and is fully consistent with the status of those Churches as part of the Holy Catholic Church. It is desired to establish a charitable educational foundation which will be true both to those characteristics and to the Catholic tradition within Anglicanism ... The object of the foundation shall be the advancement of education in the doctrines and the historical development of the Church of England and the Churches of the wider Anglican Communion, as held by those professing to stand within the Catholic tradition.

In furtherance of these aims and objectives, Affirming Catholicism is producing this series of booklets. The series will encompass two sets of books: one set will attempt to present a clear, well-argued Catholic viewpoint on issues of debate facing the Church at any given time; the other set will cover traditional doctrinal themes. The editor of the series is Jeffrey John; the first four titles in the series were: *Imagining Jesus – An Introduction to the Incarnation* by Lewis Ayres; *Why Women Priests? – The Ordination of Women and the Apostolic Ministry* by Jonathan Sedgwick; *History, Tradition and Change – Church History and the Development of Doctrine* by Peter Hinchliff; *'Permanent, Faithful, Stable' – Christian Same-sex Partnerships* by Jeffrey John. Other titles are: *Christ in Ten Thousand Places – A Catholic Perspective on Christian Encounter with Other Faiths* by Michael Ipgrave; *'Is the Anglican Church Catholic?' – The Catholicity of Anglicanism* by Vincent Strudwick; *'Making Present' – The Practice of Catholic Life and Liturgy* by Christopher Irvine.

To order these publications individually or on subscription, or for enquiries regarding the aims and activities of Affirming Catholicism write to:

The Secretary
Mainstream
St Mary-le-Bow
Cheapside
London EC2V 6AU

Tel: 071–329 4070

Preface

This pamphlet is late. It was promised months ago but the pressure of life in East London has kept pushing it to the bottom of the pile. It is important that readers should understand the context out of which it comes, a context of great social and personal stress and upheaval, of constant movement and activity, for many people a context of decay and desolation, of unemployment and racial violence, of political paralysis, of resentment and anger; and yet a context of tremendous resilience, strength and vigour. This is a pamphlet written in a hurry, under pressure, constantly interrupted by pressing needs and urgent demands.

It is just over 35 years since I first came to the East End as a student. I lived in Cable Street, scene of the anti-fascist battle of 1936. At that time a reactionary Labour Party was in power in Stepney, and on the edge of the area was some residual organised fascism. Strong and dangerous in the 1930s, the fascist presence never went away, and Mosley himself stood as parliamentary candidate for Shoreditch and Finsbury in 1965. The strongholds of the Mosley movement became breeding grounds for new groups such as the National Front (NF) which was active in the 1970s, reaching the peak of its activity in 1978. After the decline of the NF following the General Election of 1979 when its vote collapsed virtually everywhere, there was a fragmentation and regrouping within British fascism. The NF split into various groups, one of which, led by John Tyndall, became the British National Party (BNP) in 1982. It is the BNP which has formed the main fascist presence in the East End since then, and it was the election of its candidate in Millwall on 16 September 1993 and the ensuing events which brought the problems of fascism again to the surface, and which, among other things, interrupted the writing of this pamphlet.

There are deeper issues: the collapse of the East End's manufacturing base, the fragmentation and collapse of old communities, the climate of dislocation and exploitation created by the Canary Wharf development, the growth of a large, but in some areas isolated, Bengali community. The period of BNP activity has coincided almost exactly with the life of the London Docklands Development Corporation, set up in 1981; both have helped to make the Isle of Dogs known throughout the world. The persistence of unemployment, poor housing and a general sense of neglect has provided fertile ground for racist explanations.

Many of the inhabitants of the East End have not shared in the prosperity of the Thatcher years. In terms of health, the figure of 54.89 on the Jarman

Underprivileged Area Score makes it the most deprived district in the country; the chances of death here are twenty times the national average. The Spitalfields Ward is the most overcrowded ward in the UK. I work as a theologian at a centre for homeless people where we have seen an alarming increase not only in the numbers of homeless people but in the associated problems of mental illness, alcoholism, drug use, and so on.

In its political history, the East End is often portrayed as a place of extremes. It was one of the early centres of Jewish anarchism, it returned a communist MP in 1945, and it now has the first member of a fascist party as a councillor.

The BNP, like its predecessors, has exploited the vacuum created by the exhaustion and equivocation of the older parties. The power base of Labour had been built on the docks, but membership of the party had been declining for years, as had confidence in its ability to act for the people. By the 1980s this multiracial community, where one in four of the population was black, was still represented by elderly white men. Since the mid-1980s the East End has been controlled by Liberal Democrats – though of a very different political outlook to the national party which goes by that name.

I write as a revolutionary socialist who has learnt much from Marxist analysis, particularly in its Trotskyist form, and from the anarchist critique of that tradition. In contrast to much conventional wisdom I do not believe that socialism is extinct. Indeed, as opposing forces collapse, I believe that capitalism will assume more cruel and barbarous, though sophisticated, forms. Short-term prospects for an alternative to market-led capitalism, or for revolution in its usual sense, are bleak, and there is a lot of rethinking to be done by people on the left. Yet I am increasingly convinced that there is no likelihood of a smooth shift towards a more egalitarian and more just society within the present structures of capitalism of the kind that socialists in the Labour Party have favoured. This must present the church, as (actually or potentially) one of the few remaining oppositional groups, with major and painful questions. In many parts of the world, and to some extent here, it is being forced to side with poor and oppressed people, and so against the powerful and privileged. This is increasingly going to shape its future in the developed world as cities become more divided and polarised.

So this contribution to the debate on church and politics comes out of East London with its turmoil and violence, its joy and vigour, its desolation and hope for the future. It is offered as unfinished thoughts, as work in progress. It can hardly claim to be a balanced document; it is partisan, polemical, and, I hope, provocative.

KENNETH LEECH
St Botolph's Church, Aldgate
Feast of St Martin of Tours 1993

Introduction

In the 1950s the Anglican Catholic social thinker Maurice Reckitt edited a small volume, published by the Church Literature Association, called *Politics and the Faith* (Reckitt, undated). Reckitt had already made a major contribution to a long line of Anglican writing in this field, much of it under the general auspices of the Christendom Group. However, *Politics and the Faith* was small in comparison with its predecessors and was lacking in dynamism. The Church Literature Association did not show much interest in the subject matter, preoccupied as they were by then with internal ecclesiastical politics such as the validity of orders of the Church of South India. The book can be seen as a kind of last fling of one approach to politics within the Anglican community; by the time it appeared, Anglican Catholics could certainly not be seen as a radical political force, and the movement did not seem to contain many significant social thinkers who were below middle age.

Since then there have been major changes both in the political world and in the approach of Christians to it. In this pamphlet I want to attempt four things: to identify some of the key changes in the nature of the political world, of political discourse and of political expectations since the 1950s; to describe the historical contribution of Anglican Catholics to political struggle and structures, and to ask whether anything is left of this tradition; to examine some recent theological shifts in Christian engagement with politics; and to outline some issues of importance, and indeed urgency, for the church in the future.

The alarming face of modern politics

The world context

I do not intend here to look in detail at the global scene, but clearly some attention to the world context is necessary as politics can no longer be seen as purely national or local. Increasingly, decisions taken in other parts of the world affect the politics of Britain and of communities within Britain. In recent years decisions affecting the fate of people in the Isle of Dogs in East London, for example, have been made in Toronto, home of the Reichman Brothers and their property company Olympia and York. Today more and more companies and corporations are transnational rather than multinational in the sense that they have no defined national base. Individuals of a transnational kind live in cities in whose social life they have no stake or commitment. Churches, on the other hand, are multinational communities in that they seek to combine global vision with local commitment. As multinational communities, churches are bound to attend seriously to issues of a global character, yet to think and act in a transnational way, transcending the limits of the national. It is precisely here, as new forms of nationalism arise, that their most difficult political task may lie.

It is clear that recent changes in the world order will have a continuing impact on our lives. The events of 1989, with the ending of the Cold War, certainly transformed the conceptual map of the world. Many people assumed that, with the ending of the Cold War, capitalism had won, and at a superficial level this is so. Yet the Cold War did bring a certain stability, not least to Europe, for most major conflicts were fought out elsewhere. While the arms race which dominated the Cold War period has, since the Intermediate Nuclear Forces (INF) Treaty of 1987, gone into reverse as the great powers have begun to reduce their arsenals, the danger of nuclear proliferation in the Third World has assumed more serious dimensions. Now there is a danger that future conflicts will be between the First World and a nuclearised Third World. It is likely that US foreign policy will be to a large extent determined by the threat of intervention to stop alleged proliferation (Kaku and Axelrod 1987). The world since communism is seen to be a world marked by greater instability and insecurity, and there is increasing concern about the 'new world disorder'. Related to this concern is the recognition that the needs and values of capitalism are in conflict with those of the global environment. In 1992 a confidential memo from an executive of the World Bank proposed the transfer of all toxic activities to the Third World on the grounds that there was economic logic in depositing toxic waste in low-income countries, thus making the Third World a dumping ground for poisonous waste.

These crises, and those of Southern Africa, the Middle East, Somalia, Bosnia and Ireland, will continue to affect life in Britain. However, the global village does not necessarily bring about a global consciousness. It is more likely to reinforce isolation as individuals, aided by television and the trans-national media networks, exercise consumer choice in deciding what to think about within the confines of their increasingly privatised homes.

THE NEW EUROPE

It is more difficult for people in Britain to ignore the rest of Europe if only because of its physical proximity and the fact that work is more likely to have a European focus. Britain is still only precariously a part of Europe. Yet, while there is less talk today of the 'United States of Europe' of Herr Kohl or of the 'federal vocation' of M Mitterand, there is no doubt that the future of Britain is closely aligned with the European Community. The concept of European citizenship remains unclear. Indeed what is citizenship of any kind in today's world? The 'active citizen', promoted in recent Conservative policy, seems to be a description of people's leisure time work for charity rather than a concept connected with fundamental identity, rights and responsibilities. What citizenship frameworks we have seem to be more racially loaded than ever before. There is no reference whatever to race in the Treaty of Rome, and, while the Social Charter speaks of fighting discrimination, it contains no provisions as to how this might be done. Britain's weak anti-discrimination legislation is way ahead of that in other European countries. The resurgence of racism in the new Europe is extremely serious and often takes physically violent, ideologically fascist forms.

There is a growing problem of the presence of many non-citizens, people with no secure status. There are around 17 million 'third country' nationals in Europe, and many have talked of the 'social dumping' of Third World people whose cheap labour is needed but whose social position is highly insecure. Here again what is taking place in European cities is part of a world picture. A UN study has shown that 1 in 130 people in the world is now a refugee; 24 million have been displaced from their homes of whom 19 million have been forced, or have fled, abroad. Many of these displaced people are Muslims, and there is clear evidence of the growth of anti-Muslim feelings and activity in European countries including Britain. The revival of fascism is no longer a remote possibility. The Front National in France developed from scattered local power bases. Now it has 239 regional councillors, and 804 municipal councillors; in the parliamentary elections in March 1993 it gained 12 per cent of the vote. As the racist parties have grown so have racial attacks: in 1992 21 people died in Germany, and 11 in Britain, as a result of racial violence.

The politics of Britain are increasingly affected by these wider factors.

Britain: changing forms of political life

It is more than thirty years since Daniel Bell wrote of 'the end of ideology', and this theme was to become a recurring one throughout the 1960s. The term 'Butskellism' (after R A Butler, the Conservative minister, and Hugh Gaitskell, leader of the Labour Party) was coined to suggest that, on most major issues, the two parties were at one. Ideology, it was claimed, was now outdated; the future lay with pragmatism, with technical decisions, and with compromise. Bell was specifically aware of the end of left-wing ideological formulae. These were the years of disillusionment with the socialist bloc, the years when many socialists broke with the Communist Party, and when the future of the left was precarious. Many former socialists had taken the well-trodden path to the right. Bell's thesis was taken up by many leading world political figures such as President Kennedy, while in Britain Harold Macmillan offered a 'middle way', a kind of refined, human face of capitalism.

At the same time others were warning that all was not well with the world of welfare capitalism, and were seeing reality differently. Karl Polanyi argued that dependence on the market as the guiding force of society spelt the end of society in any meaningful sense. The American writer C Wright Mills issued prophetic warnings about centralised private economies, bureaucratic politics, a commodified culture, huge military arsenals and the deterioration of the human mind itself. To read many of the works of the 1950s and 1960s is to grasp in microcosm much of what has surfaced in our own day.

We have seen both echoes of these earlier debates, and also depressing evidence of the fulfilment of some earlier warnings, in recent polemics. Francis Fukuyama's thesis of 'the end of history' has received much publicity (Fukuyama 1992). Reminiscent of Bell, this view sees the future in terms of economic calculation and the solution of technical problems, such as the environment and consumer demands. Fukuyama is not untypical of the present mood. Many voices, in the USA and UK, are telling us that liberal democratic capitalism has triumphed; the war is over; so Christians, and others, must make the best of it and get what they can out of the system with which we are left. There is no alternative.

The triumph of capitalism, and the end of the socialist project, was a central theme of the Thatcher years in Britain.

THATCHERISM AND THE RETURN OF POVERTY

The growth of Thatcherism was associated both with the economic liberalism and free market ideology of the Institute of Economic Affairs and with a crude type of moral and social authoritarianism which has gradually become normative. During the Thatcher and Major years the political climate has become more rigid, more ideological, albeit increasingly, disguised under such labels as 'common sense' and 'traditional values'. More and more we have seen human rights – the right of peaceful assembly, freedom of information, education, trade union membership, local government – curtailed as the power of the executive increased.

In particular these years have been marked by the acceleration of poverty and deprivation. Of course, world economic conditions were linked to these developments, for Thatcherism did not occur in isolation from the global restructuring of companies and jobs and the resulting depression of wages, elimination of jobs and use of cheap migrant labour. So unemployment has become part of the landscape not only of Britain but of Europe and the USA. In Europe the average unemployment rate has risen from 2.9 (1969–73) to 9.5 (1990–2). The unemployed are the fastest growing category of poor people in Europe, and people are remaining unemployed for much longer. In Britain possibly one third of unemployed people are under 25.

In Britain we have witnessed and experienced a real worsening of conditions not only for the unemployed but for all of the most deprived groups in our society. The poverty line was redefined twenty-three times during the Thatcher years. In 1992, according to the Low Pay Unit, 10 million adults in Britain earned less than the Council of Europe's 'decency threshold' of £3.80 per hour. Between 1979 and 1987 the number of people receiving less than half the average income more than doubled to around 10.5 million. In 1991 a director of Tesco received an increase of £21,865 per week (over £1,000,000 per year), while between 1979 and 1988 over 5 million people, the poorest tenth of the population, experienced a fall in their income by an average of 6.2 per cent. Real living standards for the poorest million have fallen since 1980 by 10–15 per cent.

These realities have been seen by many commentators not as unfortunate accidents but as direct results of government social policy. More than ten years ago the Roman Catholic Laity Commission in its report *Community, Benefit and Taxation* (1982) observed:

> It was possible to hope, in the face of all the evidence, that things would get better . . . But now even this has changed. The present government reflects a widespread mood which does not feel guilty about the poor, and seems quite prepared to tolerate more inequality.

Many years ago R H Tawney wrote that there was nothing which revealed the true character of a social philosophy more clearly than the way in which it treated those who fell by the way (Tawney 1969). It is the increase in the numbers of such people which has marked our recent social history, and my view is that, in the continuing attack on poor people, we have seen the true face of capitalism as it casts off its refuse.

Linked with the rise of poverty has been the popularisation of the idea of an 'underclass', a concept imported from the USA. There is considerable confusion about the meaning of this term, which in the USA has both strong racial connotations and undertones of contempt. However, one section of the population which is invariably included within its confines is those who are homeless. Yet nothing is clearer from recent studies of, and experience with, homeless people than their immense variety and diversity. No longer can homeless people be classified as vagrant alcoholics, young runaways or drop-outs, terms which were always inaccurate in any case. Today we are seeing many more young homeless, male and female, more black homeless, more families, more beggars, and a growing number of middle class and professional victims of repossession by building societies. The number of repossessions grew from 2530 in 1979 to 22,930 in 1987; 70 per cent of families accepted as homeless by local authorities in 1988 were homeless as a result of mortgage arrears. If this group is an underclass, it is an extraordinarily wide class.

The truth is that what is occurring is not so much the emergence of an underclass as the breakdown of traditional concepts of 'the poor' to embrace many diverse sections of the population. It is human dignity and human value which is under threat. The crisis is one of enormous spiritual importance, and it raises the question: can it be 'solved' by conventional political approaches? Indeed, does politics as previously conceived now exist at all?

As the present régime has continued, though at first with less obvious dogmatism and an appearance of caring and humanity under John Major, it has in fact assumed more unpleasant forms of domination and arrogance. The speeches at the 1993 Conservative Party conference marked a low point in terms of the lack of intellectual content as well as the intolerance, the vulgarity, and the appeal to the lowest instincts of the membership. In one speech a well-known academic was described as a 'nutter', while the language used by another minister about 'foreigners' would have featured well at a fascist meeting. Yet at the same conference John Major called for a return to traditional values including decency, tolerance, respect, and courtesy – all features which were missing from the speeches of his colleagues. Since then we have seen the attacks on single mothers and the calls for more punitive measures to deal with crime in spite of all the evidence that such measures do not work. As political rhetoric and writing deteriorates in its intellectual content, it seems to be taken over more and more by clichés and slogans. One reviewer of the recent memoirs of Margaret Thatcher described them as filled with clichés, malice and contempt and compared them to *Mein*

Kampf (Robert Harris, *The Independent on Sunday*, 24 October 1993). So is there any hope for politics today?

In the past, the notion of 'opposition' had some clear political meaning, even though the claim that the Labour Party offered no more than a reformed version of capitalism goes back many years. Trotsky described the Labour Party as 'a kind of amalgam of conservatism and liberalism partially adapted to the needs of the trade unions'. Certainly socialism was not very important in the early history of the Party, for example between 1910 and 1924. The 1929 election programme did not mention the word at all (even though Tawney drafted it). In the late 1960s, however, the Harold Wilson era in Britain, there was a sense of hope, of optimism, even of triumph. 'Socialism is right back on the agenda' announced *Tribune*, the left-wing Labour paper, on 6 April 1966, while the Christian socialist MP Eric Heffer wrote in the same paper on 6 May 1966 that Labour could now begin to transform British society. Since then, however, the Labour Party has been in decline. Membership fell by half between 1964 and 1970, and has fallen from a million in the 1950s to around 200,000 today. A Gallup poll in 1987 showed that 60 per cent of voters did not know what the Labour Party stood for, while more recent research suggests that 25 per cent of new members are dissatisfied and are likely to leave (*The Guardian*, 25 September 1993).

The Labour Party may never form another government. Indeed, some commentators predict that, as it rose with the twentieth century, so it will die with that century. Will socialism also die? As a historical movement, socialism was wedded to the culture of modernity, and it is this culture which is now in crisis. The socialist project was based on the idea of the economy and society as stable machines, and this too is now questioned. The working class base of the movement has been eroded.

Historically Labour had its roots in the industrial working class. But in recent years we have seen the continued receding of class as a major category and focus of political thinking, combined with over-simplified accounts of its disappearance as a social and economic reality. In 1940 George Orwell described England as the 'most class ridden society in the world'. Since then, as the manual working class has declined, the numbers of unskilled service workers, and of people of indeterminate class, have increased, and we have seen the rise of professional society. While there is no basis for the 'withering away of class', about which we once heard a good deal, it is clear that the class structure is changing dramatically, and the class character of politics has shifted irreversibly. Politics is not derived from economics in a simple way. Working class trade unionists living in council houses now form only 5 per cent of the electorate; 32 per cent are working class owner occupiers. From

1964 to 1983 the traditional working class declined from 47 per cent of the electorate to 34 per cent. The Labour Party may consist mainly of working class people, but the working class is not mainly socialist. We have seen what Hobsbawm calls 'the dissolution of the political expression of class consciousness.'

So the historical and cultural underpinnings of socialism have gone. It is not surprising that whereas in 1956 the Labour politician Anthony Crosland wrote a book called *The Future of Socialism*, now we are more likely to find books and articles entitled 'Can socialism live?' or 'Does socialism have a future?' Fredric Jameson speaks of the 'decay of the very concept of social-ism', and Ralf Dahrendorf of 'the strange death of socialism'. Hardly a day goes by without some contribution on these lines. But many speak not simply of decay and death but of the need for renewal, revision, rethinking. Stuart Hall argues that we need to redefine the whole project of socialism (Hall 1988), the Socialist Society talks of the 'reconstitution of the socialist project' and the Institute for Public Policy Research of 'reinventing the left'. The Democratic Left, successor to the Communist Party, calls for a transformation of socialist thought based on a courageous facing of the depth of the crisis before it (Wilks 1993).

The collapse of the communist regimes has clearly called the whole future of socialist societies into question. For some, this marks 'the end of history', for others it represents the possibility of seeing socialism afresh, liberated from the false path of Stalinism. In Britain the negative experience of the centralised state and of local state bureaucracies – which Margaret Thatcher was able to exploit so well – has made the whole identification of socialism with central planning and state ownership questionable. This may mean that socialism itself is doomed: if it does not, it surely means that a lot of rethinking and redefining is needed. The recent Labour Party document *Looking to the Future* mentions socialism only once, and, as Joe Rogaly wrote, it 'has nothing to do with socialism' (*Financial Times*, 26 May 1990). Whether it is socialist or not, the Labour Party seems to appeal to an ageing sector of the population and to its least modern segments.

A WIDER MALAISE

However, the fate of the Labour Party is one facet of a wider malaise which affects mainstream politics in Britain. Although they have been in power, albeit through a series of minority votes, for almost fifteen years, the Con-servatives also seem both to be devoid of new thinking and to be collapsing at grass roots level, with an 80 per cent decline in membership over the last forty years (Ball and Seddon 1994). Ministers seem to know less and less about the areas they are meant to control, and their statements and interviews have diminishing content as well as credibility. Serious debate with them has become extremely difficult.

The content of current Conservative ideology seems to be an unsavoury mixture of moral fundamentalism and the economics of the 'free' market. On the one hand, everything seems to be reduced to cash transactions, and human beings are seen as consumers and customers before all else. But, as some Conservative thinkers have pointed out, there seems to be no coherent view of the functions or limits of the market, and certainly no view of the need for, or meaning of, human community (Gray 1993). So economists are now speaking of the need for more public commitment and public interest, for a new economics which transcends the free market versus interventionism debate. Of course, the market society is very untraditional and has no respect for tradition or for culture of any kind: hence the moral chaos and spiritual emptiness at the heart of our society. Yet, on the other hand, in the face of this chaos which is itself in large part the product of the idolatry of market forces, we see a crude type of moralism calling us back to the 'traditional values' of some past age. This moralism has in recent months become focused on the cry of 'back to basics'. But, like so much else in government rhetoric, it has a hollow ring and seems devoid of real substance.

There is, however, one current reality whose substance is beyond doubt and which is closely connected with the reduction of human beings to their market value. This is the increasing racism in our society. From the 1950s, when cheap labour was recruited from the Caribbean, it was clear that labour demands were not linked with any programme of racial equality. It was black people's labour that was wanted, not their presence. Now we see both the tolerance, and indeed the encouragement, of the forces of xenophobia and bigotry which are resurfacing all over Euruope, assuming explicitly fascist forms in many places. A Gallup poll for Channel Four's 'Bloody Foreigners' programme on 7 November 1993 showed that 51 per cent of people believed that racial tension was increasing in Britain. That would be serious enough in itself were it not for the additional fact that this increase has come about in part as a result of the collusion with, and failure to resist, its rise by successive governments. At the 1993 Conservative Party conference John Major trivialised this most serious issue by telling primary school teachers that they should not 'waste their time on the politics of gender, race and class'. The prospects for any wholesome view of human community, or any movement towards human equality, from Conservative sources are bleak. Nor do people seem to expect such a view; those who vote for the present regime have few if any expectations that any coherent moral progress will ensue. The most that can be expected is lower taxes and the maintenance of some degree of comfort, prosperity and safety. We have become a society whose dominant values are those of contentment and complacency.

An apolitical culture?

Many recent studies present a picture of a decentred culture, a culture with no heart, no core, no positions, no values. The report *Faith in the City* (1985) raised the question of whether there was the political will to eradicate poverty and inequality, but there is a deeper question about the nature of the political. Much modern politics, in both the USA and Britain, is increasingly a dialogue of government, business and corporate élites, over the heads of the people. In Britain it is widely recognised that Westminster is increasingly out of touch with people, so it is not surprising that a mood of anti-politics has grown up as the gap between government and governed grows wider. The 'legitimation crisis' of which Jurgen Habermas wrote in the early 1970s seems to have become ever more real.

In the USA voting has been perceived as irrelevant for many years. According to data from 1988, only 50 per cent of Americans vote compared with 76 per cent in Britain and 86 per cent in France. But in Britain by 1991 7.1 per cent of the population was not on the electoral register compared with 6.5 per cent in 1981. The Conservative John Biffen has spoken of 'a footloose and disillusioned electorate on a scale unprecedented since 1945' (*The Guardian*, 2 November 1993).

Alongside political apathy goes political ignorance. One study of 5000 16–20 year olds in 1992 described them as a generation of 'political illiterates'. According to a poll of 17 year olds in 1993, one in ten was unable to find Britain on a world map, two-thirds could not name two members of the cabinet, and less than half knew when the Second World War ended.

So are we 'losing faith in politics' (Anthony King, *Daily Telegraph*, 20 September 1993), or reaching 'the end of politics' (Martin Jacques, *Sunday Times*, 18 July 1993)? Certainly the conventional parties seem more and more cut-off from the modern world, still living in the world of simple ideologies, of hierarchical patterns and of clarity about the nature of location of power. This is an age of career politicians, people of office rather than of principle (Riddell 1993). As cliché and standardised response replace serious discussion, so it has become more difficult to distinguish left from right. Yet political debate is still stuck within the parameters of the old polarised vocabulary. So we have moved beyond the question of whether political life is unprincipled (Marquand 1988) to the question of whether it exists at all in the sense of a way of organising society through thoughtful debate and compromise rather than through war and disorder. Can there be serious political debate within our present framework? Are there common standards of rationality and of moral discourse? Or is Alasdair MacIntyre correct when he says that 'modern politics is civil war carried on by other means' (MacIntyre 1981: 236)?

One striking feature of our recent history has been the rise of political pressure groups of various kinds. From the beginning of the Direct Action Committee Against Nuclear War (which led to the Campaign for Nuclear Disarmament in 1958) to the present day, there is a long and impressive history of groups and organisations which have operated both within the parliamentary process (through lobbying and so on) and outside it (through rallies, mail order literature, mass protests, and, in some cases, civil disobedience). We also see some evidence of popular movements of protest entering into the world of the parties as in the rise, for some time, of the various Green parties. In West Germany (as it then was) in March 1986, The Greens (Die Grünen) gained 5.6 per cent of the vote and this rose to 8.3 per cent in 1987. Since then there has been a decline throughout Europe, though there is still much local activity on pollution and other environmental issues. At the local level, there has been the increased popularity of broad-based organising which began with the work of the late Saul Alinsky in Chicago. Today there are Alinsky-type groups in Bristol and Liverpool. There are many other examples of political involvement which bypass or relate obliquely to the tradition of the parties. However, single-issue politics are too narrow in their range, and while specific campaigns may have an effect, the dominant machine is able to absorb them since they offer no overall threat or alternative way forward. It can be argued that the rise of pressure groups is itself an indication of the atomised cultural fragmentation which is now so widespread as to be the norm within society. Another factor is that pressure groups are less effective in relation to their size. The small and little known groups often have more success in achieving their aims, while the large ones are forced to make use of the techniques of mail order and media appearances which do not necessarily involve effectiveness.

A wide range of vital issues are no longer capable of being addressed within the party system. Indeed the most vital issues are precisely, those which can find no expression there. In so desperate a situation, it would seem to follow that we need new sites of resistance, new spheres for political struggle.

For many years the church has played a crucial role within the political process. Is anything left of this tradition of political involvement, and can it bear hope for the renewal of politics in the future?

The 'Catholic social tradition': is anything left?

On a Catholic incarnational and sacramental understanding, lack of interest in, contempt for, or irresponsibility towards the world of politics is not possible. Of course, this attitude has its dangers, and the attraction of fascism, dictatorship and various forms of theocracy remains a danger for Catholic Christians in every age. Catholic social doctrine, where it stresses law and order more than justice and liberation, can easily move in a direction which reinforces, baptises and provides the spiritual justification for structures of oppression: Franco's Spain, Salazar's Portugal and many other examples spring to mind. But one option which is not really possible it that of other-worldliness, the piety of withdrawal aligned with a theology of individual salvation. Although such piety and theology may, for a while, characterise Catholic attitudes, just as much as those of Protestant individualists, at the end of the day they are incompatible with Catholic theology.

What is now termed Catholic social thought goes back to Augustine's *City of God*, though medieval thinkers found resources in the teachings of Augustine's contemporaries such as Ambrose, John Chrysostom, and the Cappadocians. Augustine saw that the two cities were confused and mixed together, and, while his teaching did encourage a mistaken identification of the Kingdom of God with the Church, there is no doubt that he saw clearly that Christian theology had a political aspect. It was in later centuries that a body of theological reflection developed about war, prices, interest and other social and political questions, which was to become the basis for modern Catholic social doctrine. In the Roman Catholic Church the doctrine was embodied in the works of Thomas Aquinas where we find a range of social teachings – for example, the unqualified condemnation of usury, or the insistence that unjust laws are not to be obeyed and indeed are not law at all. This tradition was later to be expounded and developed in the papal social encyclicals which began with Leo XIII's *Rerum Novarum* in 1891 and continue to this day.

Anglican Catholics shared in the earlier thinking both insofar as the English church was part of the Roman communion, and in the fact that, over many centuries, English church leaders played an important role in the struggle for justice. The late Canon Stanley Evans, in one of his papers issued from Holy Trinity, Dalston, in the 1950s, pointed out that the Anglican Church looked back to the great fighters of these years.

It looks back to the Celtic Church which served the British people in days of darkness and brought them civilization and hope.

It looks back to leaders like Theobald who brought learning and order to a divided land.

It looks back to saints like Botolph who combined land development with prayer and gave food to the poor.

It looks back to bishops like the Saxon Wulfstan who stamped out the slave trade at the time of the Norman Conquest.

It looks back to inspired leaders like Becket who defied kings in the interest of the people . . .

There are many examples of medieval bishops and priests who struggled for justice within the political arena: there was Anselm, enthroned as Archbishop of Canterbury 900 years ago in 1093, who strongly opposed slavery; there was John Ball, the 'hedge priest', who led the Essex peasants in the rising of 1381; there were thousands of unknown Christians whose political action was rooted in their faith.

All these people took for granted that Christianity involved political action, for the modern notion of a split between sacred and secular did not exist. Indeed, as Maurice Reckitt pointed out in 1935:

> If you had told any typical Christian thinker in any century from the twelfth to the sixteenth that religion had nothing to do with economics, and that bishops must not intrude in these matters upon the deliberations of laymen – propositions which to many of the correspondents to our newspapers appear to be axiomatic – he would either have trembled for your faith or feared for your reason. He would have regarded you, in short, as either a heretic or a lunatic. (Reckitt 1935: 12–13).

While, after the Reformation, establishment Anglican political thought became tied to the doctrine of divine right of kings and to the defence of the established order, the belief that Christian faith must be expressed in political terms remained within Anglicanism.

The Oxford Movement began in 1833 on a political issue: the suppression of a number of Irish bishoprics. The church–state crisis which inaugurated the movement led to a strong opposition to the interference of the state in the affairs of the church and to an assertion of the autonomy of the church as a community which antedated the state. In its commitment to this autonomy the Oxford Movement was a radical movement, and the logical end of the movement would have been the disestablishment of the Church of England. While this did not occur, a radical social and political dimension did grow up in the emerging Anglican Catholic movement within a few decades. However, we need to be careful not to read things back into this history which the evidence does not justify.

For example, there is a belief that there was once a golden age when the

Anglican Catholic movement was marked by a strong social conscience, when the parishes of 'full faith' were staffed by priests who stood within a rebel tradition. Linked with this was the picture of the 'slum priests' who were, so it is claimed, also social radicals. There is no evidence that any of this is true. It is quite wrong to see most Anglican Catholics in the formative years as socialists or social radicals. From the 1870s there was conflict between the authoritarian and the radical wings of the Oxford Movement. Athelstan Riley, writing in 1884, saw the essence of Catholicism as lying in respect for authority, and he rejected the whole idea of a 'liberal Catholic' as 'a Latitudinarian with certain sacramental opinions'. As Anglican Catholicism developed, much of it moved in a reactionary direction. Many of the clergy within the movement were pietist and some verged towards fascism.

However, as early as 1848 an alternative social theology was growing up, associated with the name of F D Maurice. The term 'Christian socialism' is sometimes used for the short-lived movement around Maurice, Ludlow and Kingsley which flourished from 1848 to 1854, but it is more commonly used of a tradition stretching from then to the present day. Maurice's influence extended way beyond the immediate context of the 1840s and 1850s, and many generations of Anglican social activists were shaped by his theology. In 1889 the Christian Social Union (CSU) was formed, one of the first organisations to be formed on the basis of Maurice's thought. It was the Christian Social Union which began the long tradition of respectable Anglican social comment. Its president, B F Westcott, Bishop of Durham, was no revolutionary. He was horrified by *Rerum Novarum* with its stress on the rights of labour, and saw the encyclical as 'revolutionary and socialistic'. Yet he did hold to a co-operative understanding of socialism, and in an often-quoted speech in 1890 he argued that socialism and individualism corresponded to opposite views of humanity. Out of the CSU came the journal *Commonwealth*, edited for years by Henry Scott Holland. By the early 1900s the CSU had permeated the church hierarchy, and many of the bishops were members. In 1920 it merged with the Navy Mission to form the Industrial Christian Fellowship, after which its radicalism was tamed and its influence subsided. The CSU reflected an incarnational approach to society, an optimism with regard to human progress, and a view of the Kingdom of God as a gradual process towards a just social order. It represented the reformist stream in Anglican social thought, deeply influenced by social liberalism, and strongly paternalist in its style – though in many respects more radical than its equivalent groups today. 1899 was the year of the Dock Strike, of the publication of *Fabian Essays*, and of the symposium *Lux Mundi* which was to provide theological underpinning to Christian social thinking. By 1900 social responsibility and a vague form of Christian socialism was broadly accepted within the Church of England; by 1920 the Lambeth Conference was calling for fundamental social change.

Running alongside this respectable stream of Anglican social thought was a rebel stream. In 1877 Stewart Headlam, the curate of St Matthew's, Bethnal Green, founded the Guild of St Matthew (GSM), which was soon to become the powerhouse of the Christian left in England. Headlam was undoubtedly the most bohemian and most controversial Anglican priest of the late Victorian age. He stood bail for Oscar Wilde and sent a telegram to the atheist Charles Bradlaugh in prison 'in the name of Jesus Christ the Emancipator'. Charles Marson called Headlam 'the bravest of captains and most skilful of the swordsmen of the Holy Ghost'. Headlam believed in the common ownership of land, the abolition of the monarchy and the House of Lords, and the creation of a socialist commonwealth. He was a strong supporter of the ballet and the music hall, for which his licence to officiate in the Diocese of London was removed and never restored, and his writings nourished a whole culture of resistance in the latter years of the nineteenth century. At the time of the jubilee of Queen Victoria in 1886, Headlam wrote:

> The Queen's Jubilee is good, but the people's Jubilee is better. Why may not the year upon which we now enter be the Jubiliee of both Queen and people? For the Jubilee of the Hebrews, as ordained by the great statesman whom God for their deliverance raised up and inspired, was the Jubilee of a whole people: and its observance was founded upon, and was expressly designed to conserve, a divinely ordained system of Land Nationalisation.

The Guild of St Matthew included among its members Thomas Hancock (who called the Magnificat 'the hymn of the universal social revolution') and Charles Marson. Marson's book *God's Cooperative Society* (1914) remains an important study of the church and its social mission and is in some ways more relevant now than it was when he wrote it. For example, it contained Marson's comments on the establishment.

> As long as our bishops are appointed by prime ministers of any belief or none, and are appointed with the first consideration that their policy should be pacific, their warfare accomplished in their curateage, so long the church militant will hold forts and man walls, but will remain ineffective in its conquest of the world (Marson 1914: 1–2).

Marson saw that 'the establishment, an absurdity in a non-Christian polity, and a disaster when controlled by mere statesmen, must be snapped from the limbs of the church' (ibid). His words, and so much more from those days, remain both valid and urgent. Indeed the GSM as a whole has much to teach us today, not least through its stress on the centrality of the ownership of land to socialist strategy, its concern for human celebration expressed in its support for the ballet, the pub and the music hall, and its willingness to get its hands dirty in the cause of justice.

The GSM gave birth to two other socialist groups, the Church Socialist League, founded in 1906, and the Catholic Crusade, founded in 1916. In both the figure of Conrad Noel was central. Noel, vicar of Thaxted in Essex until 1942, was the key figure in the libertarian socialist wing of the church for many years. Though he is sometimes claimed today by people who are termed 'Anglo-Catholic', he firmly rejected the Anglo-Catholic label, preferring to call himself a sacramental socialist (Leech 1993: 53). He recognised that there were clear divisions within the 'Catholic movement', and that, theologically, liturgically and politically, he was far removed from the ritualists who formed the mainstream of the movement. These divisions remain in our day, and Noel has much to teach us still.

Noel was a visionary and a prophet, and he saw the role of the Catholic Crusade to be, to a great extent, that of nurturing and sustaining the vision of an alternative society. 'Our principal work is not "social reform" nor pietistic exercises but the stirring within the people of the hunger and thirst for the righteousness which shall fill them with the eternal things and a due measure of the things that are temporal' (Noel 1940: 221). Linked with this visionary impulse was a strong sense of the place of art and beauty both in worship and in the building of the new order. The Crusade's Statement of Principle says: 'If you do not believe in beauty, art, dancing and song; if you believe that religion only has concern with another world; if you believe in "peace at any price"; if you wish to toady to the rich and rejoice in looking down upon the poor; we do not need your help'. More than any other group, the Catholic Crusade kept alive the elements of celebration, mirth and festivity within the Christian left. To go to Thaxted Church was to enter a new world, and to begin to experience something of the joys of the Age to Come.

In 1924 the League of the Kingdom of God was formed which soon became the Christendom Group. These groups operated at a more cerebral level than the Catholic Crusade. For many years the Christendom Group formed a resource for the study of social and political issues within Anglicanism in Britain. Among its leading thinkers were V A Demant, Maurice Reckitt and W G Peck, all of them from the more socially aware wing of the Anglican Catholic tradition. Its publications offered a persistent critique and questioning of the assumptions behind western societies, their economic life and their political styles, usually digging beneath the surface rather than addressing immediate political questions. Thus in 1947 the Group claimed that 'judgement has plainly gone forth against the sort of society of which this country was the pioneer', it drew attention to the danger of identifying church and culture, and it argued that 'the international market economy, the indefinite expansion of which was the axiomatic assumption of all orthodox economics for 150 years, has now broken down, and that this country in particular can only hope to survive by reconstructing her economy on other foundations' (Christendom Group 1947: 3, 5). The Group was often criticised for being detached from reality, and, because its material was addressed to a fairly small group of highly literate people, it is often seen as elitist and remote from ordinary concerns. But many of the issues which the Christendom Group raised are still urgent, its work of rigorous analysis and reflection is unfinished, and no similar body, except perhaps the Jubilee Group, has taken its place since it finally came to an end in the 1960s.

There were other groups of Christian socialists which worked at a more popular level, and were loosely linked with the wider Labour movement. The Society of Socialist Christians, formed in 1924, became the Socialist Christian League (SCL). In its early years it had a strong nonconformist input, but by the end of its life the London branch was overwhelmingly Anglican Catholic with a strong presence in the East End of London. The Council of Clergy and Ministers for Common Ownership (CCMCO) was formed in 1942, and was also dominated by Anglicans, mainly in the Catholic tradition. In its manifesto it put its position clearly.

Our present economic system is immoral and unChristian. Its appeal is nakedly to self interest; its technique is economic competition. It leads to the exploitation of the weak by the strong, it promotes mass selfishness, class divisions, and international war. It is a worship of Mammon, and as such is a moral outrage. This being so, it is part of the church's duty to God to say so at whatever risk of antagonising those whose vested interests lie in the maintenance of this sytem. The Son of God was manifested to destroy the works of the devil, and when something is so plainly a work of the devil, both in its principles and in its effects, nothing can excuse a minister of Christ from working for its destruction.

In 1952 the CCMCO became the Society of Socialist Clergy and Ministers (SSCM). Both bodies were dominated by the figure of Stanley Evans, who, in the 1950s, was Vicar of Holy Trinity, Dalston, in East London. While the SCL was a broad grouping containing socialists of varying colours and shades, including some anarchist communists of the Kropotkin type, the SSCM tended to follow the Communist Party line fairly closely, at least until 1956. During the 1950s members of the SCL and the SSCM met regularly in The Lamb in Bloomsbury to discuss closer co-operation, and, after publishing *Papers from the Lamb*, in 1960 both bodies merged to form the present Christian Socialist Movement. This group became much more closely aligned with the Labour Party than had any earlier Christian socialist groups, and it has, in the last few years, significantly increased both its membership and its support from Labour MPs.

These organisations, from the Catholic Crusade to the CSM, have operated at both national and local levels. Their members have been heavily involved in local struggles, particularly around housing and health questions – Charles Jenkinson in Leeds, John Groser in Stepney, Etienne Watts in Ancoats, Manchester, are well-known examples. As early as 1900 Henry Scott Holland said that London was in danger of collapse into paralysis, while Charles Marson predicted that many of the new housing blocks would decay and would be very expensive to demolish. The strength of Anglican Catholic social movements lay in their uniting of liturgy and life and in their integration of social theology with concrete local work. Today CSM branches are involved in local issues, yet all these groups are small and peripheral, and most church members are probably unaware of them.

The older movement of reformist Christian socialism reached its moment of respectability and apparent success when William Temple became Archbishop, first of York and then of Canterbury. Temple was the first person to use the term 'welfare state', and, with R H Tawney and Richard Titmuss, was one of the major architects of the post-war restructuring of British society. Temple is still remembered for his encouragement of serious dialogue on political issues within the nation and for his work in bringing together large numbers of social thinkers and activists, as at the Malvern Conference of 1941. His book *Christianity and Social Order*, published in 1942, was a best seller. Temple remained an Edwardian, nurtured by the public schools and Oxbridge; furthermore, he assumed a degree of good will and of common concern between church and government, as well as of the influence of one on the other; this world is no more.

The death of Temple in 1944 brought to an end one phase of Christian involvement in British politics. Today political action by the church is increasingly accepted, even by some Conservatives, but tends to be of a very polite and establishment kind. The General Synod sets up working parties which produce reports like *The Church and the Bomb*, and a few years ago the Archbishop's Commission on Urban Priority Areas produced its report *Faith in the City*. While there was media criticism of these reports, the general principle that the church has a right to express its views, in Temple's words, 'the right to interfere', is widely accepted. The Board for Social Responsibility and its local offshoots throughout the country are active and, within their limits, effective in such work. However, the dominant Anglican style which has characterised the church from Westcott to Carey tends to reflect and perpetuate a 'trickle down' style of political intervention offering reformist and genteel comment, filtered through the proper channels – the 'letter to *The Times*' has been its most fitting symbol. Today it is far less effective than in the past because it is based on assumptions about the political climate and process which no longer apply.

The Christian left moreover has tended to be both clerical and small, out of touch with the bulk of the 'working class movement' (itself a phrase which raises questions today) and with the world of secular political action. The social conscience and political awareness of Anglican Catholics today is weak and there is an atmosphere of nostalgia and sentimentality about the past. So Bishop Frank Weston's inspiring address to the 1923 Anglo-Catholic Congress (the 'Come out from before your tabernacles' speech) is often quoted as a way of articulating some kind of social consciousness. But such an appeal to the language of a bygone age is seductive, vague and very safe; it no longer engages with concrete issues, it is politically unreal. So does anything remain? One thing is very clear. The whole shape of Christian engagement with political structures has been transformed by the ecumenical consciousness since the 1960s; it is impossible to evaluate the present potential of Anglican Catholics without taking these changes into account.

Christians and politics: some recent shifts

Christian attitudes to political action have been going through some major changes in recent years. As increased globalisation has made a 'What benefits John Bull' attitude to politics impossible (though it survives and revives at the local level), so the globalising of Christian consciousness has meant that an insular British view of Christianity or the church's role no longer makes sense. Much of the earlier thinking of Anglican social activists showed little awareness of, or interest in, the wider Christian world. Today what happens to Christians in El Salvador or in the Sudan or in South Africa has an impact on the thinking and practice of Christians in Britain in a way that was not possible even several decades ago. Boundaries of race and nation, as well as those based upon confessional divisions rooted in past history, have started to become blurred and confused. Things which were once thought solid have melted into air. New alliances have been built, new friends discovered in strange places. Many rigid polarisations have collapsed, although, in the process of change, other types of polarisation and new divisions have appeared.

One of the effects of this ferment is that Christians who have avoided political action, or whose understanding of the social dimensions of the gospel and of ministry was extremely narrow, have changed their thinking and practice. A new generation of radical Christians and politically active Christians has arrived, and their presence has called into question many earlier assumptions and positions.

This is particularly true in the case of evangelicals, many of whom have been strongly affected by the experience of their fellow evangelicals in the Third World and in the USA. From an earlier commitment to social witness – as in the days of Shaftesbury and Wilberforce – there occurred, during the nineteenth century, what became known as 'the great reversal', when evangelicals moved towards individualism, pietism and an other-worldly theology which led to political conservatism in practice. In recent years we have witnessed and experienced the radicalisation of a whole section of evangelicals, and a rediscovery of lost elements in their own tradition. A number of dates are of critical importance here. In 1966 the Wheaton Declaration deplored the 'unscriptural isolation from the world' which had marked much evangelical life, noting in particular the neglect of attention to racism and poverty. 1967 was the year when the National Anglican Evangelical Congress met at Keele, with social concern high on the agenda. In 1973 the Declaration of Evangelical Social Concern was issued in Chicago (and so became known as the Chicago Declaration): it attacked materialism and the maldistribution of world resources and called evangelicals to a renewed commitment to social justice. 1974 saw the International Congress on World Evangelisation at Lausanne, from which came the Lausanne Covenant represented a major rejection of the divorce between *kerygma* and *diakonia*, between the preaching of the gospel and service to humanity. It was from this congress that the movement of 'radical discipleship' became known. All these were turning points in evangelical social thought and practice.

Running parallel with these developments has been the experience of evangelicals in the inner city. It was as a result of his experience in Canning Town that David Sheppard, now Bishop of Liverpool, saw that his theology needed to change in a number of crucial ways, and his path was not unusual. Ted Roberts in Bethnal Green, Neville Black in Liverpool, Denis Downham in Spitalfields, Richard Allen in Leeds – these and many others were examples of a new breed of socially active evangelicals which was emerging in the 1960s. Out of this urban experience came the Frontier Youth Trust, the Evangelical Coalition for Urban Mission, Evangelical Christians for Racial Justice, and many other groups. Powerful preachers like Jim Punton, and people with experience in non-Christian areas of the Third World like Chris Sugden, have also changed the evangelical political climate. Much of this upheaval was influenced by evangelicals in the USA such as Jim Wallis and the Sojourners Community in Washington DC. Wallis's books, such as *Agenda for Biblical People* and *The Call to Conversion*, have had a powerful impact on evangelicals here.

There has been a particular influence which has come from the Mennonites, the heirs of the Anabaptists. The publication in 1972 of John Howard Yoder's book *The Politics of Jesus* brought the Mennonite approach to a wider audience. Yoder saw that the primary social structure through which the gospel worked to change other structures was the Christian community and therefore that the social and political character of that community was of fundamental importance. Since then the writings of Stanley Hauerwas on social ethics have also shown the influence of the Mennonite tradition. Of all the Reformation churches, the Anabaptists most emphasised the ethical basis of Christian life, the importance of the disciplined Christian community, the need for resistance to injustice and to 'the world', and the centrality of the practice of non-violence. The revival of interest in this tradition, shown by the recent appearance of a new British journal *Anabaptism Today*, indicates that its neglected contribution to the Christian role in politics is now being rediscovered.

The last thirty years have also seen major changes within the Roman Catholic communion. Pope Pius XI's encyclical *Quadragesimo Anno* (1931) condemned socialism in strong terms, and for many years socialism and Catholicism were seen as incompatible. (The fact that most Roman Catholics in Britain voted Labour was tolerated on the grounds that the Labour Party was not socialist! Who said the Pope wasn't infallible?) In spite of this, there was some involvement in political affairs, notably in Cardinal Manning's intervention in the dock strike of 1889. But for the most part, in England the Roman Catholic Church saw itself as having a mission to Irish, Italian and other minority groups and had little concern with, or involvement in, political issues which were seen as English. Nor was there much public concern with international politics apart from the work of small groups such as Pax. In recent years, since the Second Vatican Council, there has been a tremendous increase in political involvement, both in domestic affairs (the Catholic Housing Aid Society, Roman Catholic involvement in Church Action on Poverty and similar groups) and in international affairs (CAFOD, CIIR, Pax Christi, etc.) This shift in Catholic practice in Britain corresponds to a major shift in the attitudes to socialism and capitalism, to war and peace, to poverty and inequality, on a global scale since John XXIII's *Pacem in Terris* (1963) and Paul VI's *Populorum Progressio* (1967).

Since then we have seen a massive growth of the Catholic left and of Catholic radicalism throughout the world. While it is the liberation theology of Central and South America which has made Catholic radicalism widely known, the radical movements in the Roman communion have been far more widespread and diverse. Moreover, in spite of attempts to control the new freedom within that communion, it is clear that the Roman communion is, and will remain, a major site for Christian political engagement for many years.

There are many other changes – the growth of a strong radical wing within Methodism with a presence in most cities, the persistent and faithful witness of the Society of Friends with constant evidence of renewal within that tradition. There has been the impact of feminism within the Christian movement, as well as the failure of the power structures within the churches to take its claims seriously. There has been the encouraging, but also worrying, growth of the 'managerial radicals' as church committees and boards have taken a number of individuals of radical hue into their bureaucracies, and so helped to sever them from their roots. There seems to have been a revival of Christian socialism in the last few years, and there is a need to build on this. And there has been a major growth of black Christianity, with the British black-led churches, mainly of Pentecostal origin, currently in a state of ferment. The major denomination is the New Testament Church of God with its world headquarters in Cleveland, Tennessee. On a global scale this is a very conservative, mainly white church, but in the inner urban areas in England it has attracted many young radical black Christians who will either transform it or leave it. The future is not clear. What is clear is that black Christian leaders such as Martin Luther King, Alan Boesak and Desmond Tutu, as well as newer figures such as Cornel West and Katie Cannon, are having an impact within traditions which have not previously been open to their message. It is clear also that many black Christians in Britain are breaking away from the racist traditions of the plantocracy which gave birth to the churches, and are rediscovering the subversive and liberating power of the gospel. The future of black Christianity in relation to British politics is open and unclear, but it is bound to be of major significance since most Christians in the inner urban areas are black. The changes in black churches will have a major impact on the shape of Christian witness as a whole.

On the negative side, we have seen the spread of suburban Christian detachment and privatism, the increased polarisation of suburban and inner urban forms of Christianity, the growth of the Christian right in its varied forms including crude and violent forms of fundamentalism, and the spread of a range of types of false spirituality and élitism.

What about Anglican Catholics? They seem to have been declining, both in numerical importance and in theological and practical seriousness. Certainly the radical wing of the movement has faded and has contributed little of any value to serious thinking within the church or the country in recent years. The recent debate on the ordination of women has exposed the worst features of the movement. Many of the individuals who have carried the Catholic label are now isolated from the movement or embarrassed to be associated with it in any formal sense. It may be that there will be a significant revival of Anglican Catholicism, that 'Affirming Catholicism' may gather the positive forces within the movement, but it seems unlikely. It is more likely that the movement as such will die in the next decade or so, but that those of its insights which are still relevant will be absorbed into the wider Christian framework. Whatever happens to the Anglican Catholic movement, there are major questions about the church and the politics of the future which must be faced.

Into the next millennium:
some matters of urgency

The Anglican Catholic movement is in a state of crisis, not just because of its own internal pathologies, but because of the profound changes which have taken place across Europe and the world. These changes have had the most profound and troubling effects on communities and on religious and political movements. Unfortunately those who are called Anglican Catholics have tended to cultivate their own somewhat precious and unreal world, a 'bubble world' as Valerie Pitt has called it, which has become more and more severed from wider networks of thought and activity. Since the 1950s Anglican Catholics have not only tended to be absorbed with internal ecclesiastical matters to the decay of the older 'social tradition', but they have also become cut off from most of the creative movements in the Christian world. The question of whether that social tradition can be renewed does not have a clear answer and is bound up with the question of whether Anglican Catholicism has a future at all.

However, whatever happens to Anglican Catholics, both political systems and faith traditions have been thrown into turmoil and have also been thrown closer together, though in states of confusion and uncertainty. Left and right, catholics and evangelicals, find themselves aligned, often against those with whom they have in the past found support and sympathy. In many inner city districts, Anglican Catholic parishes and gospel halls survive together amid a mainly Muslim population. Lines of demarcation are no longer as clear as they were and any approach to political action in the coming years must take account of the seriousness of these changes.

The churches' relationship to the political order cannot be unchanged, and must be subjected to careful scrutiny and interrogation. Yet much Christian comment on the political order continues as if this were not so. For example, much earlier Anglican social thought was based on assumptions linked to the idea of Christendom, a pan-European Christian society which, it was held, had once existed and could be restored. But is the Christendom model, so beloved by Belloc and his successors, really a viable model for twenty-first century Europe? Belloc believed that 'Europe must return to the faith or Europe will perish' (Belloc 1920: 186), and there is evidence that something akin to this view is held by Pope John Paul II. Such a view discounts not only the significant Jewish and Muslim communities within Europe but also the major impact of post-Enlightenment secularism. Can this really be written off as so much diversion, a false path, a mistaken project? Are we to campaign for a new Christendom?

Whatever the answer to that question, it is clear that Europe and Britain are no longer predominantly Christian communities. Church leaders, nationally and locally, who appeal to a national constituency will find themselves speaking more and more to a residual minority. But is there a way in which Christians, whether leaders of churches or not, can address the public arena? I believe there is, but that there needs to be a thorough study of, and reflection on, the changed character of the public arena, its areas of commonality and of conflict, its potential for discovering common ground, and so on. This process needs to happen locally as well as nationally, since areas differ dramatically in terms of the relationship between church and community and in terms of their cultural and religious make-up. Without such concrete analysis, a style of Christian social witness rooted in a past understanding of the nature of society will be quite ineffective.

Again, much Christian social and political thought has been influenced by the tradition of liberalism, that body of thought and practice which played such an important part in the development of British political life. One of the assumptions of the liberal ethos was that reform and change were possible by negotiation and good will, without conflict or too much pain, and that there was a common reservoir of good will to which all parties in the nation would subscribe.

The report *Faith in the City* is a good example of both the strengths and the limitations of the older liberal tradition. It assumes a general good will, takes for granted that we are all on the same side. At the very beginning of the report the authors tell us of the 'basic Christian principles of justice and compassion which we believe we share with the great majority of the people of Britain' (ACUPA: xiv.) This assumes that there is a common body of compassion and of the 'compassionate character' of society and excludes from the outset any possibility that Christian principles and vision might be in conflict with those of the dominant society. And this determines the character of its approach. For if we are all on the same side really, then conversion and challenge are not needed, merely a nudge, a reminder, gentle persuasion at the most.

There is still much in that liberal tradition which we can take with us into the next millennium, but we need to beware of perpetuating a style which was always precarious and which is now not viable. Many church leaders are still living in the world in which a quiet word in the ear of the Prime Minister, or a polite meeting with a cabinet minister, would have its effect. But today such liberalism is an illusion. We are in a post-liberal epoch, and a new age is upon us.

So there are serious problems with this approach, and with campaigns and struggles based on it. The church has taken for granted for too long that reforms are possible within the existing framework. The entire basis of the establishment, and of the 'trickle down theology' which goes with it, rests on the belief that the present system is reformable. I have never believed that this is so or that the attainment of justice and equality is possible without a major onslaught on capitalism and its entire framework of values. If the church of the future is to have credibility and strength in the struggle with evil in the social and political realms it must disaffiliate from the establishment, the monarchy and the financial and economic structures with which it is bound up. Of course, it is sensible to use what resources the establishment offers as long as it lasts – that is called 'making friends of the mammon of unrighteousness' – but this must go hand in hand with a commitment to end it. Such a commitment to disaffiliation and liberation is essential to the church's integrity and fidelity to the gospel. The present economic crisis in the Church of England, for example, could be good, and may well be the work of the Holy Spirit. So we need a more rigorous theology of disaffiliation, of disengagement, of resistance, of liberation. Those who collude with Babylon will share in its collapse. Deliverance and renewal lies on the other side of captivity.

Again, one of the weaknesses of much Christian social and political criticism has been an assumption that the church was on neutral ground in pronouncing judgement on the injustices of the world. The message 'Physician, heal thyself' was not heard. There was little concern to turn the lens onto the structures of the church itself, and it was when Leonardo Boff did so in his critique of the Roman Catholic Communion that he got into trouble. Clearly, there are many issues which will continue to confront the church and determine its political priorities. The black Christian writer Cornel West lays special stress on such issues as a more egalitarian redistribution of wealth and resources, the continuing attack on racism and white supremacy, the need to push back patriarchal and homophobic structures, and the need for a cultural renaissance. But all this depends on the ability and will within the church to face these disorders within its own structures.

It is hardly surprising that, as many Christians seek to interrogate the past and discern the way ahead, new and more aggressive kinds of fundamentalism should have appeared. Fundamentalism arises when traditions are in crisis. It has been described as an attempt to act traditionally as if the crisis had not occurred, yet in another sense it is deeply untraditional for it narrows down the character and content of faith to certain rigid positions. In the past much fundamentalism was of an other-worldly and 'spiritual' kind. Today fundamentalism is rampant and profoundly political, no less so because its politics belong to the far right. From its origins in the USA before the First World War, when it arose as a protest against evolution, socialism and liberal theology, it has always been closely linked with violence. The dangers of fundamentalism are only too evident, and as cable TV and other forms of technology spread, the influence of the Christian right will be felt in Britain. Protestant fundamentalism of the USA is only one facet of the revival. We are also seeing the resurgence of some of the older and more unpleasant forms of right-wing Catholic fundamentalism in Europe. Nor is the phenomenon restricted to the Christian tradition.

Fundamentalism presents a way of relating religion to politics which must not only be avoided but strenuously opposed. It is a deranged form of Christianity, a pathological growth of a highly dangerous kind; in some ways it forms a more serious threat to the Christian faith than secular atheism. But the evidence of deranged forms of politicised religion is not an argument for some form of apolitical religion; apolitical religion strengthens and upholds the status quo. We need to find more humble and more thoughtful forms of political action, forms which derive from the character of the Christian community itself as a community of justice, love and peace.

There is no doubt that there will be major political questions in the coming years which will affect national and local churches and will demand organised political responses. We need to learn from and build on the success of such pressure groups as Church Action on Poverty, and, unfortunately, it is clear that its work will become more urgent in the next decades. Equally there is no doubt that the church will, in the coming years, be forced to take up more positions which are in conflict with those of the government. Indeed, in the present state of the Labour Party, the church has become the effective opposition, and it needs to accept that as a God-given position for a time. But it is essential that the church's political role is not one of simply responding to government measures and positions. The present government is quite skilful at setting the agenda and inviting responses which deflect attention from other urgent matters, for example, the recent focus on single parents which took place while a number of pits closed. The church must not be caught out by such tactics. This requires both vigilance and awareness of what is happening, but it also requires an offensive and pre-emptive strategy. The struggle for a just society calls for more than responsiveness.

During the Thatcher years, it became clear that the government's understanding of the social and political role of the church, and indeed of Christianity itself, was quite different from that of church leaders and most well-informed Christians. This gulf continues. It is in part due to a serious ignorance about Christianity on the part of the government, an ignorance for which churches in the past are partly responsible; in part, it is due to the tendency of all governments to want religion to cement and reinforce the stability of the civil order; and in part it is a result of the influence of a particular kind of Protestant individualism on the present régime. One common view is that the church's primary concern is with 'morality', and that poverty and housing are 'social' and not 'moral' issues. Douglas Hurd, in an address to members of the General Synod on 10 February 1988, regretted that the church was often concerned with 'lesser matters' – it had spent much of the previous day attacking the poll tax! Its true role was 'to rebuild moral standards and values which should form the sure foundation of a cohesive and united nation'. Hurd put the same point in an article in the *Church Times* of 9 September 1988: there were separate spheres; clergy could express their views on political and social issues but had no particular competence to do so; equally politicians might '*trespass* on the church's *home pitch* of moral guidance' (my italics) but had 'no special authority' to do so. More recently David Maclean, a Home Office minister, complained of the church's neglect of morality and of its concern with 'special issues such as housing' (*The Guardian*, 26 November 1993).

There is no space here to deal with these claims and the underlying theology except to say that they are completely mistaken, and the church will have to spend some time repudiating them. It should not, however, spend too much time on this since this would play into the government's hands and would deflect energy away from more urgent issues. In addition, some – though not all – government spokespersons are intelligent enough to know that what they are saying is nonsense, and one should not waste energy telling them what they know perfectly well. What is clear is that the church is in danger of being too polite and too timid when it needs to be far more aggressive and realise that it stands on firm ground, theologically and politically.

Perhaps it needs to be stressed that churches in the future will need to carry on and strengthen their ministry of advocacy and defence of the vulnerable. This will certainly include single parents, lesbian and gay people and Asian communities under attack. But as the process of stigmatising and scapegoating of individuals and communities continues it will include a much greater range of people throughout the country. The practice of the corporal works of mercy is bound to be seen increasingly as an act of resistance. Both in its national and its local presence, the church must take sides, and this will involve some honest facing of problems, and a clearer understanding of many matters which have not been faced. For example, my personal view is that it is important for the church to build alliances with the progressive forces within Islam and with groups opposing religious and moral intolerance. Such groups – for example, Women Against Fundamentalism which unites in opposition to religious fundamentalism across faith traditions – will become increasingly important. In an article published after his death twenty-five years ago, Thomas Merton wrote that the need to preserve the integrity of the human person in the face of totalitarian threats to human dignity was 'the most important task of the Catholic intellectual' ('Christianity and Mass Movements' in *Cross Currents* 93, 1969).

A number of vital issues in our society will continue to call for Christian action. Of course racism will present a very specific challenge to the church as will the growth of fascism in Britain and elsewhere in Europe; alliances must be built with the churches and anti-racist groups in Europe. Whether the church will be able to transcend its deeply rooted gynophobia and make a more creative contribution to the struggle for women's equality remains to be seen. Certainly the ordination of women to the priesthood will not of itself bring this about, and there are worrying signs that the recognition of women's ministry is taking place in a very apologetic and half-hearted way – though nobody in the hierarchy has yet publicly apologised to women for their treatment in the church over centuries. Whatever happens here, sexual politics will figure prominently as the defence of 'traditional values' assumes more sinister and reactionary forms. The church of the future will need to defend and uphold sexuality as a divine gift, and repudiate the new manichae-ism which is now with us. It will also need to focus more and more of its attention on poverty, housing and homelessness; and there will be so much else.

There is, however, in relation to issues such as homelessness, a real temp-tation for churches in the current political climate to accept the role of ambulance workers, picking up the pieces, offering crisis intervention and administering sticking plaster ministry. The church's task is to care for the poor; the government's task is to ensure that there are enough of them for the church to care for. Churches have always been better at comforting the afflicted than at afflicting the comfortable, happier as servants and carers than as prophets. As government attacks on the poor continue, and the welfare state suffers further erosion, the struggle for a just society will force the church to the centre of the political arena. The government will do all that it can to encourage the ambulance role, offering financial incentives and government grants to churches which limit their ministry in this way. We do well therefore to remind ourselves of Canon Percy Widdrington's warning, delivered to a conference of the Church Socialist League at Coventry in 1913.

> The church has been too long the Church Quiescent here on earth, content to serve as the scavenger of the capitalist system. If it refuses the challenge, it may survive as a pietistic sect, providing devotional opportunities for a small and dwindling section of the community, a residuary solace for the world's defeated, administering religion as an anaesthetic to help men to endure the hateful operation of life, an ambulance picking up the wounded, entered on the Charities Register – an institution among institutions. But it will cease to be the organ of the Kingdom, building up the world out of itself: it will have abandoned its mission and become apostate.

The prospect which Widdrington foresaw so long ago is more real today than when he said those words, and his challenge is more relevant.

So, finally, what are some of the implications of all this for method and strategy?

First, we need to move away from vague notions of 'social concern' and 'general principles'. We need to be aware of the deep fear of conflict within the church, and of the way in which we misuse the language of 'reconciliation'. Groups like Affirming Catholicism could become very nice, liberal, polite and 'middle Anglican', steering clear of all the dirt and mess of political struggle.

Secondly, we need to develop detailed expertise and detailed analysis, drawing on the very considerable resources and expertise among church members. We need to become far more acute in our access to information. Because of the way in which the press is controlled, and because it is increasingly difficult to recognise truth in the midst of propaganda, we need to put a lot of effort into building up alternative sources of information and analysis and into creating an alternative media. We will not be starting from scratch for there is a lot already being done by small networks, and we need to pool resources; we can learn a good deal from the monitoring of parliament by the Society of Friends, or the effective data collection and pressure group work done by Shelter, the Catholic Institute for International Relations, and the Churches' Commission for Racial Justice. Networks such as the Jubilee Group, which runs on a shoestring, need to be developed, expanded, imitated and made more efficient. We need to use journals like *Searchlight*, *Lobster* and the *Runnymede Bulletin* to keep up to date with developments on race and racism. The new socialist journal *Red Pepper* needs support and help. We need to build on and use parish magazines far more effectively as forces for justice in our areas. In the 1950s, without modern technology but with a skilful use of photography, Father Joe Williamson used his parish magazine in East London powerfully in his campaigns for slum clearance and improved housing conditions. We need to discover sympathetic journalists and researchers. All this calls for a far more efficient and organised use of our resources, which, in spite of recent financial troubles, are still better than those of most similar organisations.

Thirdly, we need to start with very concrete issues. There needs to be thorough and ongoing research on local issues. The local church must become an organising force for analysis, reflection and struggle.

Fourthly, churches need to act together as units. We need to develop the theme of the church as an alternative social reality, a rational and moral community, a centre for debate and controversy. Local churches need to keep vision alive and nurture hope in the midst of darkness and despair; they need to be communities of resistance and of celebration. We need to recover the liturgy as a prefigurative action and to nurture inspiring new forms of musical culture; no vigorous movement for political change can survive long without poetry, song, dance and the rhythms of resistance.

Fifthly, there need to be alliances between churches and other groups. The recent spread of broad-based organising of the Alinsky type in Bristol and Merseyside has its dangers and needs to be carefully scrutinised, but it has considerable strengths and long experience in mobilising people. As more and more people are frightened of speaking out because of threats to their jobs, the local church will find that it has to speak as a voice for the new 'voiceless' – bureaucrats, social workers, local authority employees. The organisation and mobilisation of the middle class in city and suburb will be one of the most arduous tasks of the church of the future: without this, no liberation theology can emerge in a society where the poor are not the majority.

Finally the church must recognise and use its minority status in British society. In 1947 Demant wrote: 'The church is not the people but a minority body in an increasingly secular environment' (Demant 1947: 60). A politically active and aware church must be theologically competent, prayerful, watchful and rooted in a profound spirituality. It may be small but it can play a crucial role as small groups often do. We need to remember Conrad Noel's words:

> The flame of truth and justice was kept alive in all ages by heroic souls who were content to be persecuted and scorned as quacks and heretics; sometimes they protested against the accepted theology of their age, sometimes against its political corruptions. There small groups are in every generation the salt of the earth, and without them a living orthodoxy will be stifled by dull conventionality (Noel 1940: vii.)

Bibliography

Stuart Bell and Anthony Seldon (eds.) (1994), *Conservative Century*, Oxford University Press.

Daniel Bell (1962), *The End of Ideology*, Glencoe, Free Press.

Hilaire Belloc (1920), *Europe and the Faith*, London, Burns and Oates.

Christendom Group (1947), *Crisis and Reality: A Christian Judgement Offered to Church and People*, London, SPCK.

V A Demant (1947), *Theology and Society*, London, Faber.

Jean Dreze and Amartya Sen (1990), *Hunger and Public Action*, Oxford, Clarendon Press.

ACUPA (Archbishop's Commission on Urban Priority Areas) (1985), *Faith in the City: A Call to Action by Church and Nation*, London, Church House Publishing.

Francis Fukuyama (1992), *The End of History and the Last Man*, London, Hamish Hamilton.

John Gray (1993), *Beyond the New Right*, London, Routledge.

Jurgen Habermas (1973), *Legitimation Crisis*, Boston, Beacon Press.

Stuart Hall (1988), *The Hard Road to Renewal*, London, Verso.

Stuart Hall and Martin Jacques (ed.) (1989), *New Times: The Changing Face of Politics in the 1990s*, London, Lawrence and Wishart.

Irving Louis Horowitz (ed.) (1963), *Power, Politics and People: The Collected Essays of C Wright Mills*, New York, Oxford University Press.

Michio Kaku and Daniel Axelrod (1987), *To Win a Nuclear War: The Pentagon's Secret War Plans*, Boston, South End Press.

William Keegan (1992), *The Spectre of Capitalism*, London, Hutchinson Radius.

Kenneth Leech (1992), *The Eye of the Storm: Spiritual Resources for the Pursuit of Justice*, London, Darton, Longman and Todd.

Kenneth Leech (ed.) (1993), *Conrad Noel and the Catholic Crusade: A Critical Evaluation*, Croydon, Jubilee Group.

Alasdair MacIntyre (1981), *After Virtue*, South Bend, University of Notre Dame Press, and London, Duckworth.

David Marquand (1988), *The Unprincipled Society*, London, Cape.

Charles Marson (1914), *God's Cooperative Society*, London, Longman.

Conrad Noel (1940), *Jesus the Heretic*, London, Religious Book Club.

Maurice B Reckitt (1935), *Religion and Social Purpose*, London, SPCK.

Maurice B Reckitt (ed.) (undated), *Politics and the Faith*, London, Church Literature Association.

Peter Riddell (1993), *Honest Opportunism: The Rise of the Career Politicians*, London, Hamish Hamilton.

R H Tawney (1969 edn.), *Religion and the Rise of Capitalism*, Harmondsworth, Penguin.

Margaret Thatcher (1993), *The Downing Street Years*, London, HarperCollins.